Becoming

HER

Again

Becoming

HER

Again

Reclaim your identity, rediscover your joy,
and rebuild your confidence in the middle
of motherhood's beautiful mess.

ELYSE FRANK

For my daughters.

May you always know that becoming never stops.
And you are allowed to grow into yourself as many times
as you need.

From One Mom to Another

Hey girl,

Can we talk for a minute?

Motherhood is freakin hard.
But it's also one of the most beautiful things I have ever experienced.

It fills your heart in ways you never imagined possible. But it also stretches you, exhausts you, and asks more of you than you ever thought you could give. Somewhere between loving our children deeply and carrying the weight of everyday life, many women begin to quietly lose pieces of themselves along the way.

The feeling of loving your children more than anything in the world... while quietly wondering where parts of *you* went.

Motherhood changes everything. Your time, your priorities, your body, your relationships, and sometimes even your sense of identity. It stretches your heart in ways you never imagined. It teaches you a kind of love that is fierce, protective, and overwhelming in the most beautiful way.

But it can also be incredibly hard.

Some days feel magical—the laughter, the tiny hands reaching for yours, the moments that make your heart feel like it might burst from how full it is.

And other days feel exhausting.

The constant responsibility. The invisible mental load. The feeling of giving everything you have and still wondering if it's enough.

Somewhere between caring for everyone else, keeping the house running, and trying to hold it all together, many of us slowly begin to disappear without even realizing it.

I wrote this book for the woman who feels that tug.

The woman who is grateful for her life and her family, but still senses that she's meant for more. The woman who remembers who she used to be and wonders if she can ever feel that strong, confident, and alive again.

And the answer is yes. You absolutely can.

For a long time, I believed that becoming a mother meant certain parts of me had to be put away. My ambitions. My independence. My voice. I thought sacrifice was the only way to prove I loved my family enough.

But over time, I realized something important.

Becoming a mother didn't erase who I was.
It challenged me to rebuild her.

And if I'm being completely honest, writing parts of this book felt a little like therapy.

You know... the kind you do after your husband says something that makes you stare at him for a full ten seconds in silence.

Just long enough for him to realize he probably should have said something different.

But somewhere between the laughter, the frustration, and the late-night writing sessions, I started rediscovering parts of myself again.

This book is not about escaping motherhood. It's not about choosing yourself *instead of* your family. It's about learning that you are allowed to grow, evolve, and rediscover yourself while still loving your family deeply.

You are allowed to want more joy.

You are allowed to rebuild your confidence.

You are allowed to become the next version of yourself.

If you see yourself somewhere in these pages, know that you're not alone.

Maybe you picked up this book because a small part of you is ready to come back to life.

And maybe, just maybe, this is the moment where you begin becoming **HER again**.

With love,
Elyse

Table of Contents

Introduction

You can be a great mom, love your family fiercely, and still feel completely lost—and that doesn't make you a failure. It makes you human. And the truth is, no one hands you an instruction manual for motherhood. You are basically thrown into a world of sleepless nights, unpredictable emotions, and tiny humans who depend on you for everything. All the Pinterest boards in the world couldn't tell you exactly what to do.

Here's the deal: this book isn't a "mom manual." I'm not here to tell you how to be the perfect mom because, let's be honest, "perfect" is overrated and, more importantly, doesn't exist. Within these pages, you won't find color-coded schedules, meticulously balanced meal plans, or tips for keeping your toddler entertained while maintaining your sanity. I'm not going to tell you to create a colorful chore chart or which routine you should follow.

What I will do is give you questions to ask yourself, along with moments for self-reflection. Grab a highlighter and a pen so you can mark the parts that resonate with you. At the end of each chapter, you'll find "heart-to-self" reflection questions, prompts meant to help you pause, process, and check in with yourself. Throughout this book, you'll also find space for you to write your own thoughts if you'd like. Think of this as a place to pause, breathe, and keep all your growth in one spot.

I've found that writing these down and repeating them to yourself can be incredibly powerful. You can jot them in the space provided, stick them on your mirror, or leave them somewhere you'll see them often. For a while, my husband and I even did this together. He bought these mirror markers, and every morning we'd write down three things we were grateful for so we could start the day with a more positive mindset.

Before you begin, I want you to know this book wasn't written to be long or massive. I know who you are. You're a mom. Who even has time for that? I'm sure your brain is already full of all your other bucket list items for the day. You don't have to sit and read this uninterrupted for hours, and honestly, neither did I when I was writing this. I found random times where I could sit down and write, often pushing cleaning aside and leaving the house a wreck.

Packed with practical tools, mindset shifts, and encouragement to navigate motherhood and relationships, this book will remind you that you can be both a devoted mom and a woman reclaiming her life. Read this during nap time, while hiding in your closet, before bed, during school pick-ups, or while you're drinking your coffee. Motherhood is already demanding enough; this is here so you can read it when you can, highlight what resonates with you, and come back to it when needed.

This book is not about achieving perfection. It's for you if you love your kids deeply but sometimes miss the woman you were before motherhood. If you've ever felt guilty for wanting more, exhausted from carrying it all, or unsure how you lost yourself while building a life you're grateful for, this book is for you. It's for the moms who are doing their best and still feel like something is missing.

My reflections on motherhood are real. They are raw. I know I'm not the only mom who has felt lost, alone, and like they are drowning in motherhood. I decided to share my journey to help other women find themselves and learn to "live again" inside the madness.

Becoming HER Again was born out of the mess: sleepless nights, self-doubt, identity loss, and the quiet ache of wondering where "I" went after becoming "Mom." This book is for the women who love their kids fiercely but need permission to feel, to fall apart, to rebuild, and to rediscover who they are beneath the endless piles of laundry. Through stories, personal reflections, and raw honesty, I want to show you that a full, imperfect life is not the same as failure. You can be both: the mom in chaos and the woman finding her way through it.

I love my family more than anything. Being with my kids has given my life a whole new meaning. The world is so big, scary, and fun for them, and it's been an amazing journey seeing life through their eyes. They are the heartbeat behind every word here. I wrote these chapters because I want them to grow up and see a mother who didn't give up on herself—a mother who didn't settle for serving only others but chose to live.

No marriage is perfect, and no parent is perfect. My husband and I took what we knew about marriage and parenting and tried our best to make it work. He has made me want to tear my hair out, but he has also comforted and supported me in ways I never could have imagined. There have been moments where we loved each other deeply and moments where we misunderstood each other completely. Even on the days that feel like we are just getting by, I can't imagine doing life with anyone else. You see, parenting is just as new to him as it is to me. It's all about learning and unlearning and seeing each other through new eyes every time our situation shifts. But we work on our relationship every single day, and, most importantly, we work on ourselves. Because we can't give our all to someone else if we're not happy with who we are as individuals.

I want you to know, you don't have to have everything figured out to be worthy of love, from others or from yourself. At the end of the day, this book is about not having it figured out—and showing up anyway. *Becoming*

HER Again is for the moms who love without limits but don't want to lose themselves to motherhood. For those who look in the mirror and see a stranger, but also a spark of the woman they used to be. Give yourself permission to be imperfectly human.

As you read, there's one question I want you to keep coming back to: *If you gave yourself permission to become her again, what might change, not just in your family, but in you?*

CHAPTER ONE

Thriving on Stress
(Or So I Tell Myself)

The Cost of Always Holding it Together

It's Saturday morning. After a disagreement with my husband, I told him I needed some time alone. Life feels overwhelming lately, and I wanted to get out of the house—by myself. So here I am, sitting in a local coffee shop, sipping a cappuccino. I take mine with oat milk, a light swirl of whipped cream, and a sprinkle of cinnamon. There's a line stretching to the door, multiple conversations humming around me, a few kids running about, and people quietly tapping away on laptops. I notice the way the espresso machine screeches every few minutes, how the barista moves as if she's done this a thousand times. Looking out the window, I watch cars come and go in the parking lot. The wind makes the trees sway back and forth. It's cloudy, but thankfully, no rain is expected today. I'll take it. I'm alone, free to do as I please.

A twinge of guilt hits me, knowing my husband is at home with our kids. But I really needed this solitary moment and this cappuccino. I'm not a daily coffee drinker, but over the last few months, this little ritual of having a cappuccino on Friday or Saturday mornings has become my guilty pleasure. Do I need it? No. But something about holding a warm cup in my hands, taking slow sips, feels like a tiny oasis of calm. And being here, really being here, taking deep breaths, watching the world around me, is my reminder to slow down.

I don't live a celebrity lifestyle. There are no nannies or in-home chefs, and I certainly don't have a private jet to come and go as I please. However, I'm fortunate enough to be a stay-at-home mom while also running my own online personal training business. My days are full of taking care of the kids and their needs, client check-ins, one-on-one sessions, cooking meals, wiping asses, creating social media content, feeding the dogs, grocery shopping, meal prepping, and everything in between. A lot, right? Girl, don't I know.

Make no mistake, being a stay-at-home mom doesn't mean I have more time. My days are full, my attention is split, and most things I do are done while multitasking or being interrupted. Time for myself is something I have to create intentionally. If you're reading this and wondering when you're supposed to fit you in, I promise, you're not alone.

While my husband is at the office, I'm all hands on deck. When he comes home, I'm cooking dinner while washing dishes, getting the girls ready for an afternoon activity, and trying to keep the peace between my kids when attitudes are flying around. Alone time for me looks like my twenty or thirty-minute workout at 6:15 a.m., crossing my fingers my kids don't wake up earlier than expected. But we all know they can sense when Mom is awake. (Yes, this includes my husband, too.)

Before my second daughter started preschool, she was home with me all day, which changed my routine a little. If I didn't get my workout in early, I'd try to squeeze it in during the afternoon, whether she was awake or napping. Getting a workout in, even if it's interrupted, is a necessity for me. It's not just about fitness; it's about keeping my sanity. Working out helps me reset, feel grounded, and show up as a better version of myself.

I'm a big believer in bringing your kids into your workouts. Yes, they can be distracting, and your workouts may take longer, but life doesn't pause just because you want to move your body. My daughters constantly climb on my back while I'm in a plank position. They laugh and think it's a fun game, and I get to strengthen my core. Sitting on my stomach while I do glute bridges is another favorite of theirs.

My oldest daughter is now in kindergarten, and my three-year-old is in preschool three days a week until 11:30

a.m. On occasion, I send her to lunch, and suddenly I get an extra hour. But by Friday mornings, I'm craving a reason to leave the house. My reason right now is writing this book. My Monday, Wednesday, and Friday mornings are now the time for me to create this journey.

Before my kids started school this year, they would tag along on my little coffee shop adventures. Some days we visited the same spot, other times we went somewhere new. They usually requested smoothies, so we had a mini routine: start at the coffee shop to order my matcha or cappuccino, head over for smoothies, and end at the bakery for a croissant. We sit together, make small talk about our surroundings, and share laughs while they inevitably make a mess with their snack. Oh, and you know we are making a pit stop at Target because no outing is complete without one. Going in for three things and somehow leaving with a full cart and zero memory of what those three things were.

I'm grateful for the time I get to spend with them. I realize not every mom gets the chance to stay home, to witness every milestone, or to have these little outings on a Friday morning. Their little voices and their sweet smiles constantly remind me how much I love being their mom. And yet, for a while now, I've felt like something was missing in my life.

On top of being a full-time in-home chef, house cleaner, and nurse, Uber driver, and event planner (I'm pretty sure I should update my resume), I'm also a certified personal trainer, certified women's fitness specialist, and pre-and-postnatal certified coach who trains clients virtually every week. Mom life gave me many titles, but I earned these certifications through hard work and dedication.

I love helping others with their fitness journeys and pushing them in workouts. I owned a fitness studio for several years until the world shut down because of COVID-19. Trying to navigate all the social distancing restrictions, constant rule changes, and fears of being in a gym setting was brutal. Classes were canceled, memberships dropped, and every week felt like a new hurdle I didn't know how to jump.

I was a new mom during a pandemic (my first daughter was born in April 2020), trying to keep a business afloat with so many obstacles and barely any income—and it was breaking me. I was carrying the weight of motherhood, financial stress, and the heartbreak of watching something I loved slowly fall apart. I had to constantly remind myself that what was happening wasn't my fault. There were things completely outside of my control, even though it still felt like I was failing. I ended up having to sell my business, a long and painful story that will remain in my past—one of those chapters that still stings to think about. I lost a piece of myself along with that business. I questioned my worth, my strength, and whether I'd ever feel like me again.

But what I didn't realize then was that losing that dream was making space for a new one. One that looked different, but still allowed me to help women, move my body, and build a life that fit this season of motherhood.

That season knocked me down hard, but it didn't end me. It reshaped me.

Looking back, despite how hard that time was, I believe the universe had other plans for me. Between being a mom and juggling everything else, I'm not sure how my husband and I would have made it work. Losing the studio gave me space to focus on motherhood, build my online training brand, and figure out what life had in store for me. But five years and two kids later, I still feel like my cup isn't full.

Seated in the coffee shop, a hundred things related to my chaotic life are running through my head. But first, let me check Instagram to see if anyone commented on my post. (We all do it, so don't judge me.) Twenty minutes slip by as I scroll through everyone else's seemingly perfect lives. Meanwhile, at home, laundry waits to be folded, my husband left his dishes in the sink from breakfast, the kids are arguing over toys in the living room, and the dog is barking wildly on the patio because she smells food on the counter.

It's like my brain has all these sticky notes just floating around, reminding me of my "do not forget" list. Don't forget to switch the laundry. Don't forget to order the birthday gift. The list goes on. Breakfast dishes need cleaning, the kids need snacks packed, I have to create reels for a brand, plan dinner, and oh my God, why are there toys everywhere? Okay, take a deep breath. Have I even had enough water today?

When I sit down and try to breathe, there's constant noise playing in my head. No one but me knows it exists. It's the mental load mothers carry quietly, a weight invisible on the outside, but always sitting there on our shoulders. We put so much stress on ourselves and then wonder why we end up closing the closet door, sitting on the floor, and crying it out. (And if you haven't done that yet, just wait, it's coming.) Sometimes an ugly cry on the closet floor is exactly what I need to pull myself together and get back out there in the wild.

There's no denying it, being a mom can blur the woman you used to be. Honestly, I could cry right now just thinking about it. I used to be a woman who showered whenever I wanted, without opening the door five times because I thought I heard someone crying. It would take me hours to get ready because I was jamming to music and singing. I drove around listening to whatever music I wanted without restrictions, and I could shop anytime without distractions.

As mothers, we try so hard to do it all, carrying the weight of everything on our shoulders. I'm not one to ask for help; I don't want to hear "no" or have to explain why I can't just do it myself. So I throw on my big girl pants and figure out how to fix things myself. It is constant stress, and even when I get a moment to myself, something else demands my attention.

Who doesn't love reality TV? There are times when I watch these shows, and I realize my life isn't that bad. At least I'm not surrounded by backstabbing friends, lies, or couples yelling in public. Honestly, thank you, reality TV, for making me feel a little better about myself. But let's be clear, my life is far from perfect. On a Friday night, I'll switch over to a Hallmark movie and suddenly find myself wishing my husband would scoop me off the couch and dance with me in the living room, the fireplace glowing behind us. I want to ask him, but can't he just read my mind? What a romantic surprise that would be.

Despite the chaos, I love being a mom and a wife. I love the little family my husband and I have built and the life we share. So why can't I just let go of trying to "fix" the chaos and simply learn to live in it? Why is letting go so hard? Why can't I just let the playroom look like a tornado has rushed through?

I joke around and say I thrive on stress, but honestly, I do because I'm used to it. That little voice inside my head reminds me what the house will look like and how

I will feel if there isn't some sort of organization. It's that constant battle back and forth in your head. What if one small change felt like a breath of fresh air? What is it about trusting that everything will be okay that we struggle to release?

As I sit there a little longer than I planned, feeling the weight of my cappuccino get lighter and then slowly disappear, I begin to wonder. How many women are sitting in coffee shops just like this one, holding cups they don't really need, searching for a moment that feels like their own. How many of us are pretending these small escapes are enough, because admitting we need more feels too risky? We don't want to sound ungrateful. We don't want to seem like we're failing at something we love so deeply.

This moment won't fix anything. It won't empty the dishwasher or quiet the noise waiting at home. But for now, it reminds me that I exist outside of my responsibilities. And maybe the harder work isn't fixing the chaos, but learning to trust who I am without trying to control it.

Heart-to-Self Moment

When was the last time I allowed myself to step away without rushing or feeling guilty?

That moment looked like:

Who was I before life became this loud? What parts of her do I miss?

One part of the old me I still feel connected to is:

What is one small way I can create space for myself this week?

This week I will:

CHAPTER TWO

Fighting the Voices
The Noise Between Who I am and Who I Want to Be

It warms my heart when I have clients or friends tell me how much I have impacted their lives, how my energy is contagious, or how I motivate them to work out—or even just wake up with a positive mindset. I'm not afraid to put myself out there. But there's another side of me that holds back. I have all these ideas swirling in my head, all these things I want to do, but I never actually sit down and plan them out. Every time I try, something pulls me away. My kids need me for something, or the house needs cleaning, or I need to get to the grocery store. It's like the thought of stepping away for one day somehow creates more work.

Even something as simple as dinner with my girlfriends can turn into a mental marathon. Before I can even think about getting ready, I have to make sure dinner is ready for my husband. I find myself making sure everything is set up so it's easier for him when he gets home from work, even if that means I'm late getting ready and late to dinner. Don't get me wrong, there are times when he'll just say he can order dinner, and obviously that helps. But still, there's this constant pressure on me just to be able to go out and enjoy a night with my friends. I know this is something that falls on me too, and I'm learning to speak up and say, "You've got to figure out dinner tonight." I'm realizing that I don't have to solve every problem, all the time.

Have you ever heard Jana Kramer's song "Voices"? If you haven't, give it a listen. Do it when you get a moment alone. Maybe while you are driving to the store, during your kids' nap times, or while you are sipping your morning cup of coffee, and it's still calm and quiet. Just sit there and really listen to the lyrics. She starts out saying, "I am strong, I am beautiful," then follows with, "I'm fighting voices in my head." And it's so true. Every single day, I feel like I am constantly fighting those same voices in my head, the ones that overanalyze and overthink my new ideas, listing everything that could go wrong until I talk myself out of it.

These voices make me question my own worth. I find myself constantly trying to make things better for everyone else, even when I should be prioritizing myself. It's like I instinctively take on the weight, pain, and stress of others and carry it as if it's mine. But in doing that, I push my own needs and dreams further down the list. My head constantly bounces back and forth between what I want to do and what I should do.

Despite the inner voices that fill me with self-doubt, I still have moments when I feel empowered and strong. I remember that I am worthy, that I do deserve that trip I've been wanting to take. I remember that I can have my own identity, and one outside of "mom status." And that's really where writing this book began. Because I know I'm not alone in this. There are so many women in the world who are going through the same thing. Whether you are a stay-at-home mom, a working mom, or a single mom, we are all fighting those inner voices.

So, I want you to hear this: You are beautiful, you are strong, and you are doing amazing, mama!

We all are, even on the days we don't feel empowered or worthy. We have to keep reminding ourselves that on the days we feel overwhelmed and guilty, everything will work out. Somewhere along the way, I learned that being a "good" woman meant being everything for everyone else. That saying yes made me helpful, reliable, and worthy. And saying no, even when I needed to, felt selfish. No one ever said that out loud, but it became a belief I carried anyway.

There are moments when I look back and think I could've handled a situation better. I could have counted to ten instead of yelling at my daughter after she did something she had already been told not to do a thousand times. And then the guilt hits. Why do I feel so terrible for reaching that boiling point?

You know the point I'm talking about. It starts off calm, you try to stay patient and give your kid a chance to explain themselves. You reason, you talk it out, you remind them what they did wrong. But then suddenly, the switch flips. They throw themselves on the floor, crying uncontrollably. You try to comfort them, go in for a hug, but they twist and kick and scream even louder. You've tried everything to help them process their feelings, but it's like nothing works. And then it happens: you can feel your blood rushing to your head, veins popping out, your patience slipping away. You finally snap and yell—loud. Your throat burns, your voice cracks, and for a split second, everything goes silent... except your own heartbeat pounding in your ears.

Then the crying starts again—only louder this time. You look at your child's face and realize your scream scared her, hurt her, and now she's crying harder than before. And the heavy, gut-wrenching guilt washes over you. Now look at us. Both crying, both overwhelmed, both just trying our best. When the room is quieter, and our breaths have slowed, I pull her close. I tell her I'm sorry I yelled. I tell her that moms have big feelings too, and sometimes we mess up. She nods, wipes her tears, and leans into me like nothing is broken. And maybe nothing is.

Since moments like this, I've worked on myself. Not because I think I should never raise my voice, but because I want to pause before I do. I've learned to recognize the signs before I reach my limit, to step away, take a breath, lower my tone, and try again. I don't always get it right, but I'm more aware now. More intentional. And every time I choose repair over shame, I'm showing her that love isn't about being perfect, it's about coming back and being open to talking it out.

One thing I've always promised myself, ever since I had my first daughter, is that I will not let myself believe I'm a bad mom. I know I'll mess up. I know things won't always go the way I want. But I also know I'll keep working on it, every single day. It's like anything else in life: you learn from your mistakes, and you grow. So the next time you feel like you did something wrong, don't tell yourself you're a bad mom—because you're not. None of us are perfect, and there's no "right" way to parent. Even after the hard moments, your child just wants you. You give them a sense of comfort and security that no one else can. When they call your name and ask you to play a game with them, sometimes they just need a few minutes of your time. From what I hear, there may come a day when they don't call my name or want to do things with me.

Knowing this doesn't mean the guilt disappears. Even when I remind myself that I'm doing my best, there are still moments when I question every choice I make. The smallest decisions can suddenly feel heavy, like they carry more meaning than they should. And that's usually when the guilt sneaks in, not in the big moments, but in the everyday ones.

There are times when my daughter asks me to play dolls with her, and my instinctive response is, "Not right now, I need to finish these dishes." Then I watch her play by herself, and suddenly, I'm feeling guilty for washing the freaking dishes. But if I don't do them, they'll pile up in the sink and stress me out later. Then the questions start: Does she feel like I don't love her now? Did I just miss a moment that matters? What's the right thing to do here? And yet, there are also moments when I drop everything, crawl on the floor, and let the world wait. And those are the moments that remind me that connection doesn't require perfection, it just requires presence.

Looking at it through a different lens, my daughter isn't going to remember how clean our kitchen was. She's going to remember the times I sat on the floor playing Barbies with her. The times we went outside together to check the garden. The moments that made her feel seen. But she's also going to learn how to be independent when she plays by herself for a little while, so that I can wash the dishes. I've just gotten so used to doing chores after every meal so they don't pile up, but maybe that's where I can start to give myself a little grace. Perhaps I can learn to let go of some of the pressure I put on myself to "get it all done." Because sometimes letting a few dishes sit in the sink is exactly what I need to feel a little less pressure and a little more peace.

When other moms come to me for advice, I step right into it. I know exactly what to say. I lift them up, remind them of their strength, and boost their confidence without hesitation. From the outside, I look like I have it all together, and maybe on most days, I do. But what they don't see is that I'm fighting my own battles too, quietly navigating the same doubts and pressure in my own head. I remind them to rest while pushing myself to keep going. *THAT'S who I am*, I thought. I want to take the weight off your shoulders, carry the pain with you, and give you everything you need to feel supported.

I'm starting to see that the voices in my head get louder when I'm under too much pressure. The pressure to be everything, to fix everything, to never fall short. Maybe it isn't confidence I'm lacking, or strength I need to find. Maybe it's peace. Because in the moments I let go, even just a little, the noise softens. The doubts don't disappear completely, but they never stop shouting. And maybe that's the shift. Less pressure. More peace. Enough quiet to remind myself that I'm already worthy, even on the days I feel overwhelmed.

Heart-to-Self Moment

What inner voice holds the most power over me right now?
My weakness is:

Where in my life am I putting pressure on myself to "fix it all" instead of allowing myself to be human?
The part of my life I try hardest to control is:

How could I choose grace over guilt the next time I fall short?
When guilt shows up, I want to try:

CHAPTER THREE

The Invisible Struggle

The Exhaustion Behind the Strength

Most of my days start before the sun's even fully up. My typical day looks like:

* Wake up around 6:15 a.m., get myself together for the day (sorry, not a 5 a.m. girl.)
* Make my daughter's lunch while mixing my morning supplements
* Get a workout in (if time allows)
* Make breakfast
* Train a client
* Take my daughters to school
* More clients, errands, house chores, and/or appointments
* Pick up my youngest mid-morning
* Work on client programs while keeping my two-year-old entertained
* Pick up my oldest around 3:30 p.m.
* Head to after-school activities or sports
* Cook dinner, clean up after dinner

* Give the girls baths and get everyone ready for bed
* Check what's on the calendar for tomorrow
* Watch a show (if I can keep my eyes open)
* Pass out. Goodnight!

Wow you guys! Somewhere in the mix of all that, I wrote this book. Go me!

We all know that with kids, no two days ever look the same. Some days, things flow. Everyone's happy, the house is (somewhat) clean, and you feel like you're crushing it. Other days, it's messy, unpredictable, and far from Instagram-worthy. But that's life in the noise; you make it work, even when it looks a little ugly.

Some mornings, I'm answering client messages with one hand while making eggs with the other, a backpack falls off the counter, and a dog barking because she needs to go out, all before 8 a.m. And somehow, this has become normal.

So how exactly do we handle a demanding and ever-changing to-do list and still end each day feeling grateful, happy, and accomplished?

We give ourselves grace.

Not every day is going to go the way we hoped. Not every choice we make will be the right one. We can't fix everything, and we can't prevent the storms of daily life. But we can do a better job of "living in the moment." Let your kids figure things out. Let the dishes pile up. Go to the coffee shop by yourself and don't feel guilty for seeking a few hours of alone time.

I'll admit something: sometimes I talk myself out of asking my husband for time to myself. Here I am, trying to better myself and feel like my own person, but struggling to even ask for "me time." Why can't my husband just come out and tell me to take a break while he handles the kids? Yet even when he does, I freeze and don't know what to do with myself.

That's the invisible part no one really talks about. Not just the workload, but the silence around it. The way you carry everything so well that no one thinks to check if you're tired. The way you tell yourself it's easier to just keep going than to explain what you need. Over time, that silence starts to feel heavy. Not because anyone is doing something wrong, but because you've stopped giving yourself permission to be honest about what you're carrying.

Like lying in bed at night, exhausted but with a racing mind, replaying tomorrow's schedule, wondering if you remembered spirit week, if you RSVPed, if you're out of conditioner, carrying a list no one else sees.

Come on, girl. Get it together and just say you need some time! There's nothing wrong with taking a break. In fact, it's one of the best things we can do for ourselves. Feeling overworked and overwhelmed can lead to burnout, or even resentment of our partner.

What I'm learning is that I don't need to earn rest by finishing everything on my list. Taking a break doesn't mean I failed the day; it means I respected my limits. My energy is one of my most valuable resources. When it's depleted, everything feels heavier. When it's protected, even the hard days feel manageable.

I'm realizing that asking for time isn't a weakness and isn't selfish. It's honest. It's necessary. And it's something I have to practice, even when it feels uncomfortable. My husband isn't a mind reader, and no one else is either. If I don't speak up about what I need, I'll keep carrying more than I should, and eventually, that weight turns into resentment.

I used to believe that slowing down meant falling behind. That if I stopped moving, everything would unravel. Taking care of my energy isn't about escaping my life. It's about staying connected to it. When I keep pushing past my limits, I lose patience faster, joy feels harder to access, and even the good moments feel rushed. Slowing down doesn't make me lazy; it makes me more aware.

When I allow myself space to breathe, I'm more patient with my kids. I'm more present with my husband. I'm kinder to myself. And that kindness ripples outward in ways I didn't expect.

So here's what I want you to know: you're allowed to pause. You're allowed to step away, to sit in silence, to go to the coffee shop alone, to rest without explaining yourself. You don't have to do it all to be worthy of joy or gratitude. Some days, the most productive thing you can do is protect your energy. Sometimes that looks like saying no to one extra commitment. Other times it's choosing an earlier bedtime, a quiet coffee alone, or letting the laundry wait until tomorrow. It doesn't have to be dramatic to be meaningful. Because when you take care of yourself, it doesn't mean you show up as less for your family—you show up as more. And that's something worth choosing, again and again.

Heart-to-Self Moment

When was the last time I asked for help or time for myself?
If I didn't, what stopped me:

____

____

____

What parts of my day drain my energy the most, and which ones restore it?
Drains:

____

____

Restores:

____

____

When I think about taking a break, what emotions come up first? Guilt, fear, relief, or resistance?
Or is there something else:

CHAPTER FOUR

Still Standing

Keeping it Together, Even on the Days You Feel like Falling Apart

You're still standing, and that counts for more than you realize.

Some days, I don't want advice or perspective. I don't want a solution or a silver lining. I just want to cry. Not because something terrible happened, but because everything feels heavy all at once. The kind of heavy that doesn't need a reason, it just needs space. You know it. I know it. There isn't always a reason. No argument, no bad news, no breaking point. Just a moment where the weight of everything catches up to you.

I constantly remind myself how lucky I am. How strong I'm supposed to be. How much worse it could be. And somehow, that makes me cry harder, the tears coming quicker. After talking with friends, I'm quickly reassuring myself that so many women are carrying the same quiet weight. We live different lives, our struggles don't look exactly the same, but we are carrying the same ache. The same exhaustion. The same hope that someone sees us.

On the days I want to cry, I let myself. And in that moment, it's enough to remember that I am not weak, I'm not failing, and I'm not alone.

Right now, I'm crying just writing this. I'm prob dehydrated AF (and if you're wondering, yes, that means as hell) because I haven't had a sip of water in what feels like hours. But these tears aren't just from overwhelm, although writing a book can be absolutely overwhelming. They are from joy and excitement, but also the connection I hope to have with you as the reader.

If you needed permission to feel this today, here it is. This chapter is your moment to pause. To take a breath in. To release some pressure and simply exist where you are.

Take a look at the woman staring back at you in the mirror. Who is she? And when was the last time you really saw her. Look at her with kindness Tell her you love her.

You don't have to be strong right now. You don't have to have answers. Just have to breathe.

Close your eyes. Take a deep breath in. Exhale slowly. Let it all out.

Heart-to-Self Moment

When was the last time I paused long enough to feel without trying to fix anything?

A moment I didn't rush through was:

Who reminds me that I'm not alone, even on the hard days?

Someone who reminds me I'm not alone is:

What would it sound like to speak to myself with more softness?

Instead of criticizing myself, I could say:

CHAPTER FIVE

Presence Over Perfection

Memories Matter More than Getting Everything Right

The holidays used to stress me out beyond belief. You know how it goes—the back-and-forth, multiple different houses, attending and hosting, and squeezing in everyone else's expectations. Before kids, I made it all work—every party, every dinner, everyone else happy. But now, I want to slow down. I want to watch my kids open their presents on Christmas morning while I drink a mimosa in matching pajamas, Christmas music playing in the background, laughter filling the house. I don't want to feel rushed or have to explain to my kids why they can't play with their toys because we have to get ready to leave.

I once heard a phrase that changed my life: *Your husband and kids are your immediate family. Everyone else is extended.* Let that sink in for a moment.

It's true, and it gave me permission to live the way I want to live. We can enjoy Christmas morning at home without the guilt. We can take a vacation without inviting the entire family. I can prioritize spending time with my husband and children and making memories.

Memories are everything, especially since you never know when tragedy could strike.

I was young when my parents split up. My dad had injured his back at work so badly that he couldn't work anymore. My parents argued all the time. My dad was on so much medication, and it always felt like he was just... messed up. I was young, so I didn't fully understand what was happening. Eventually, they split, and my dad went to live with his mom.

One morning, when I was thirteen, my dad showed up at our house before school. My mom told me to go outside to see what he wanted. That moment, that day, is one I still relive in my mind.

I could tell he was upset. He gave me a hug and said, "You're never going to see me again." Give me a second while I take a deep breath and cry just writing that.

I asked him where he was going, tears streaming down my face, and he said he didn't know. I went back inside to tell my mom. My life changed forever that day.

After school, I came home to my mom crying. My dad had tried to commit suicide. He was in the hospital, his body covered in third-degree burns. My mom didn't let us see him. Not a sight anyone wants to witness. At the time, I wasn't happy about it, but I can't imagine seeing him for the last time in that way.

We spent that night at my sister's house, and everything felt quiet in a way I had never felt before. The next morning, we received the news that my father had passed away in the middle of the night. Not something any kid at thirteen wants to hear or can even process. I kept thinking, Is this even real? My mind kept going back to that last moment he and I shared. If I truly knew that was going to be our last interaction, I would have tried harder to change the outcome. I would have hugged him longer. I would have said more, told him how much I loved him.

It took me a long time to forgive him for what he did, leaving his family to live life without him. At first, I thought, "How selfish," and was so angry. I cried, wondering why he left me here. Why did he choose to go when I still needed him? But as I got older, I realized that was the choice he made. He was in pain, physically and mentally, and was trying to escape the hurt he didn't know how to carry anymore. He was hurting in ways I couldn't understand at thirteen. From that experience, I've grown into the woman I am today. I am not mad at him for what he did. It taught me how fragile life is, how deeply love runs, and how important presence truly is.

Why am I telling you this story? Because it has colored everything I see and do in life, especially when it comes to my own family. Sometimes, when my husband comes home from work, I wonder why he can't just put his phone down and play with the kids. There I am, sitting on the floor, building blocks with the girls, and he's caught up in something else. It doesn't happen every day, but when it does, I can't help but wonder: What if he didn't have tomorrow? What if he didn't get to see them grow up? What memories will my kids have of their dad? I hesitate to say anything because I don't want him to feel criticized or like I think he's neglecting them. But then the other voice in my head says, "Remind him to be present." Be in the moment.

I know what I went through, and I have this picture-perfect idea in my mind of what I want my family to look like. Because it's what I always wished for with my own family. Now, I have the chance to make it right, to show my kids what love really looks like. Losing my dad taught me that life is short, and it could be taken away any day without notice. When I'm out here living my life, I have the fear that it could be my last day. I don't remember all of the memories I have of my dad because the trauma has hidden them. I refuse to let that happen to my own kids. I run around like a chicken trying to give them a happy life. Even though my own family feels messy at times, that's family, right? Everyone has their issues. But it's still love.

This is where I recognize I need to take a step back. I need to focus on my relationships with my kids and my husband, and I can't get caught up in wanting him to be perfect. Because I, myself, am not perfect. I constantly strive to make peace, to make sure everyone is okay. My husband tells me all the time to stop trying to "fix" everything. But it's my nature. It's who I am. The experiences I've had with my dad and my family have shaped me into the person I am. I'm trying so hard to live a magical life, to make everything feel perfect, that I put way too much pressure on myself. And I know it.

Looking back at my past, I see how my experiences shaped me—the pain, the loss, the moments of fear and helplessness. But I also see how those moments taught me resilience, empathy, and the importance of presence. They remind me why I show up for my girls every day, why I want to be fully engaged, and why I work to create the family I always wished for.

I'm learning that parenting isn't about perfection. It's about presence. My daughters won't remember the dishes I washed or the times I yelled. They'll remember the Christmases we spent happily together, not worried about anyone else. The vacations we took. They'll remember the times I was there with them.

And that is more than enough.

These next few questions may feel hard to answer. You don't need to have the "right" words. Sometimes saying things out loud, or writing them down, helps us understand what we actually need.

Heart-to-Self Moment

What past experience may be shaping how I show up now?
One experience is:

____

____

____

Are there traditions or expectations I've been holding onto out of guilt rather than joy?
An expectation I feel pressured to maintain is:

____

____

____

What are the moments with my family that feel the most meaningful?
The most meaningful moments to me are:

____

____

____

CHAPTER SIX

Small Wins, Big Impact
How Tiny Choices Change Everything

We don't always have all the answers, and that's okay. But sitting and doing nothing, letting the mayhem consume your whole life, definitely isn't the answer. There are things we need to fortify us, both as moms and as individuals. As moms, we need each other to lean on, and to learn, grow, smile, and laugh. And why is it that when we meet up with other moms, we always end up talking about our kids? It happens every time. We use this time to get away from them, but we end up talking about them: what they did that upset us, what made us laugh, or how their little imaginations make no sense. But honestly? It's the cutest thing watching them grow into their own little people, with big attitudes, might I add. And as individuals, we need to reconnect with ourselves and the women we were before becoming parents. How do you reconnect with yourself and feel great while "mommying" in chaos?

It's all about the small wins with big impact.

Some days, you go on a shopping spree. Everyone knows retail therapy is the best therapy. I personally love shopping for shoes. Boots, wedges, heels, sandals—it doesn't matter. DSW, here I come! But in all seriousness, sometimes it's the little things that help us feel human, not like a bum in sweats and an oversized shirt. A girl's brunch or a night out with your spouse or family, putting on your makeup, picking a cute outfit, feeling confident, glowing, and alive. Behind motherhood is a woman who still loves enjoying an espresso martini on a Saturday night, while wearing an outfit she bought five months ago.

What if you could feel that way every day? All it might take is a little foundation and mascara. You don't need a full face of makeup, just enough to cover the bags under your eyes (I've got those too) and feel a little more put together. But perhaps makeup isn't your thing. Maybe all you really need is that morning shower or an outfit with some style, instead of a typical oversized shirt and leggings. Maybe what you need is to book that haircut or finally get your nails done, something small that helps you feel like *you* again.

You don't have to go anywhere. You don't have to dress up and wear a ballgown or impress anyone. This isn't about how you look to the world, it's about how you feel when you look in the mirror. Tell yourself you're beautiful, be grateful for another day, and decide you're going to make it great.

We all know how a fresh haircut or a new set of nails instantly lifts your mood. It's kind of like when we go through a breakup and immediately think about a drastic new look for our hair. (Don't say you haven't done it, or at least haven't thought about it.) You just want something that will put a smile on your face and remind you that you've got this. This ritual is for you, not anyone else. (And yes, lazy Sundays and yoga pants are still allowed.) So choose one thing: a shower, clean clothes, a haircut, a fresh face, and let it be your way of showing up for yourself.

Some days, I curl my hair, put on a full face, and my husband asks, "Where are you going?" Literally nowhere, just the kitchen to make breakfast. But at least I'll look hot-ish for myself. And yes, I do it for him too. I refuse to let myself go completely.

Here's a little trick to get a win early in the day: put on your makeup, pick a cute but comfortable outfit, and then make your bed. I love making my bed because it's one thing I know I can accomplish every day. At night, my bed looks comfortable, calm, and still. No matter how the day went, I have a space to unwind.

Making time to work out is also incredibly helpful to me and helps keep me sane in the chaos. If you're on the edge of your seat thinking about getting started on your own fitness journey, I see you, Mama. The hardest step is the baby step, the one where you tell yourself you're ready to put this into action. I'm not expecting anyone to go from never working out to full-on gym addict overnight. It can be as simple as getting out the stroller and walking with the kids, or moving your body at home without any equipment. Maybe you've never enjoyed working out, or maybe your body doesn't move the way it used to. Maybe you're dealing with injuries, chronic pain, postpartum recovery, or mobility limitations that make certain exercises feel unrealistic. Movement doesn't have to look like running 10 miles or lifting heavy weights to failure. It can be gentle stretching, a short walk, or dancing in the kitchen. And if fitness isn't your thing, that's okay too. The goal is to connect with and care for your body, wherever you are now.

As a personal trainer, fitness has always been close to my heart. I first started taking it seriously during a moment of depression before having kids, when I realized I couldn't control everything going on around me. That experience helped me open my own fitness studio. There's no better feeling than completing a workout, lifting heavy weights, and challenging yourself with burpees.

I know firsthand that as moms, we don't always get a full workout, or we have to work out while the baby plays on the floor. But I am proud to show my kids that Mommy enjoys working out. It's not a chore; no one is making me do it. It's something I love doing for myself. Working out gives me the energy to keep up with my kids because, let me tell you, keeping up with a five-year-old at the playground, playing soccer, or running around the house like a maniac... exhausting. (And yet, somehow, they still don't want to go to bed at 8 p.m.)

Still think you have no time for a workout? If you have twenty minutes to scroll Instagram or TikTok, you can find twenty minutes to prioritize your health! You're not expected to become a "fitness mom". You are just finding one small way to care for yourself so you can feel stronger, steadier, and more like you. And while caring for your body is one powerful way to pour back into yourself, it's only one piece of the bigger transformation motherhood brings.

Motherhood hits fast. And it hits hard. One moment, you're reclaiming yourself in little bursts, a quiet coffee, a quick workout, putting on makeup just because, and the next, everything shifts. That woman who loved spontaneous adventures, binge-watching TV on rainy days, or heading out for happy hour without a second thought? She's still in there... but now, a tiny human is depending on you for everything. Your priorities, your routines, even your body— everything becomes part of this new world. When that little bundle arrives, it's not just a role shift; it's an identity shift.

You're no longer just you. You're Mom. And that shift? It's terrifying, life-changing, messy, and beautiful all at once.

Taking care of yourself, even in small ways, isn't selfish; it's necessary. It fuels you to be the mom, wife, and woman you want to be. So let this be your reminder: you're allowed to take up space in your own life. You're allowed to nurture yourself the same way you nurture everyone else. And when you do, you're not taking anything away from your family, you're giving them the best version of you.

Heart-to-Self Moment

How does my mood or patience shift when I take a few minutes for myself?
   Changes I notice:

____

____

____

What kind of movement would support my body right now, and what would "enough" look like for me this season?
   Movement for me could look like:

____

____

____

What small ritual helps me feel more like myself when life feels chaotic?
   A small ritual that helps me feel more like myself is:

____

____

____

CHAPTER SEVEN

The Shift from Womanhood to Motherhood

The Transformation No One Prepares You For

I don't know about you, but I loved being pregnant. I loved every stage, from that first pregnancy test to the random 3 a.m. bathroom trips, the little belly kicks, even the moment I had to push to get my little bean out. How incredible is it that our bodies can grow a human being and create that unexplainable connection? When my first daughter was born, nothing else mattered in that moment. The excitement, the joy, the unconditional love—it was magical. Every cuddle, every late-night feeding, every milestone mattered. The good days, the bad days, everything in between. I was amazed that I got to give life to another human and guide them through this world.

In those early days of motherhood, while you are in love with your baby, you also start to realize that everything around you feels like it's no longer "yours." You need permission to leave the house, to go to the bathroom alone, to get a workout in. (I know I'm not the only one who gets irritated when their spouse comes home and says, "I have to pee, can you watch the baby?" Umm, who watches the baby when I go? What about when I'm home alone?) In those quiet moments between feedings, diapers, and spit-ups, you start to notice changes. Your clothes fit differently. Your reflection feels unfamiliar. You miss feeling strong, energized, and confident in your body.

You start to wonder, Will I ever get my body back? How do I lose the baby weight? When will the "mom pouch" go away? Looking at yourself in the mirror after birth can make you feel strange, lost, ugly, swollen, or just... disconnected. Sleep-deprived, hormonal, and with a baby depending on you, it's easy to slip into your husband's sweatpants and forget yourself. Being a personal trainer helped because fitness has always been part of my life, and my postpartum journey. I worked out through both pregnancies, and that foundation made my postpartum recovery manageable. But some days, I'd work my ass off in workouts and not see the results I wanted quickly enough.

My boobs experienced their own journey. Prior to kids, I was a comfortable C cup, reliable and predictable. Then pregnancy came along and gave me full, perky, show-stopping boobs like a Victoria's Secret angel. And then... postpartum. As I began ending my breastfeeding journey, fourteen months with both girls, my precious gems started going downhill. The once glorious, angel-worthy boobs began to settle into their new identities, carrying the stories of motherhood, sleepless nights, growth spurts, and cluster feeds. They might not be Instagram-worthy anymore to some, but they're mine, and I've come to appreciate the story they tell. They remind me of what my body did, what I survived, and who I became in the process.

Okay, quick rant for a second. During those long nights, if the baby was up crying, my husband's go-to solution was always, "Just put a boob in it," like I hadn't already been sitting in her room for forty-five minutes feeding while he was lying in bed, sleeping. There were many times I wanted to whack him with a pillow, but I just cursed his name under my breath instead.

Being in a postpartum body is challenging. Jeans don't fit. That pouch is still there. But here's the key: stop chasing the "old body." Start building a new one. Kids can join you for walks, push-up contests, or even playful races around the house. Take breaks when needed, be patient, and focus on creating strength and confidence, little by little. It's worth the time. And most importantly, learn to enjoy the journey, enjoy motherhood, play with the baby, and celebrate little wins.

In addition to a new lifestyle and a new body, motherhood has brought me a new understanding of strength—both physical and emotional. Two months after my second daughter turned one, tragedy struck. I was on a trip with my husband for his work when I received the most devastating news: my mother had passed away. I was on a bus when my sister called. At first, I couldn't understand her, and then it all hit at once. I was an emotional wreck.

I was in another country, far away from my kids, whom I just wanted to squeeze so tight. There I was, surrounded by a bus full of conversations and laughter, and I wanted to curl up and disappear. The shock, the helplessness, it just stabbed my heart so hard I felt like I could barely breathe. The bus slowed as we arrived at our destination. Everyone stood up and grabbed their bags to head out. Life was still moving forward as if nothing had just changed forever for me.

There I was, fully tensed up, forcing myself to hold it together while hiding the truth. Inside, my world had stopped. I was tense from head to toe, trying to process the truth, but the tears came anyway. There was so much unknown, and everyone was asking if I wanted to leave to get back home, but that wasn't what was best for me. I stayed in Mexico because that's what my mom would have wanted.

I grieved the entire trip, but in a completely different way than I would have at home. Before you judge my decision, please know there was a snowstorm the next day; it would have been a 12-hour travel day, and my family needed to make decisions that night. We decided to cremate her, just like my dad, and I didn't feel the need to see her body beforehand. I wanted to remember her from the last time I saw her.

As moms, we make sacrifices and decisions that we feel are best for our kids. My mom knew she was sick but didn't tell a soul. Her passing was sudden to us, but she knew it was coming. She had stage five kidney failure. Finding out from her doctors was a shock to my family. But she didn't want to put that burden on us. Deep down, she knew we would be going crazy, and we would stop living our lives to comfort her.

She continued to live her life how she wanted— seeing her grandkids and spending time with her family. I can't imagine walking around with such life-changing news for several months and keeping it all to myself. But if there's one thing this has taught me, it's how strong my mom was. She woke up every day, knowing it could be her last, but still wanting her kids to keep living their lives. How can anyone be mad at the decision she made? Because at the end of the day, it was her decision. Her voice. Her wishes. I can't even say I wish she had told us, because I would have dropped everything. I would have been a mess.

Losing my mom changed so much in my life. Our relationship hadn't been perfect. There were arguments, doubts, eye rolls, but she always answered my calls. Even if I wasn't looking for advice, I could call just to vent. Grieving the loss of my mom, while also being a mom— that's something I can't even explain. Hearing my kids say "mom" every five seconds right after I lost mine was a hard pill to swallow. First, I had to explain what had happened to my oldest, who was only three years old at the time, and answer the questions she fired at me. The days and weeks after, the constant reminders; I just cried all the time. But there was one thing that kept me going through it all.

Strength. It's a word that defines moms in a way the world doesn't always see. Not just the physical strength it takes to carry a child or push through exhaustion, but the mental and emotional strength that keeps us moving when everything else feels like it's falling apart. My mother is the perfect example of that kind of strength. She protected us even when it meant carrying the weight of her own pain alone. She kept her fears quiet, even when she knew her time was limited.

We didn't always get along. She made me mad more times than I can count. She wasn't the overly affectionate, "I love you every day" kind of mom. But the way she chose to leave this world... that was her love. That was her power. She showed me that motherhood means showing up, even when you're hurting, even when you're scared, even when you feel like you have absolutely nothing left to give. There is something deep within us, an instinct, a fire that ignites when our children need us. We keep going. We rise. We fight because that's what moms do.

Heart-to-Self Moment

When did I first feel like I was no longer "me" and had become just "Mom?"

The moment I realized I lost "me" was:

What parts of my old life (before kids) do I miss the most?

Things I miss:

How has motherhood made me stronger, softer, or different from what I expected?

I didn't expect motherhood to make me:

CHAPTER EIGHT

The Truth about "Mom Guilt"

Breaking Free from Impossible Expectations

Mom guilt: that heavy, invisible weight we carry around without even realizing it. It creeps in quietly, whispering that we're not doing enough, not patient enough, not present enough. It shows up when we raise our voice, when we forget something at school, or when we choose to fold laundry instead of playing Barbies. And somehow, no matter how much we do, it never feels like it's enough. Mom guilt has this way of making us question our worth over the smallest things. But what I've learned is that guilt isn't always the enemy. Sometimes, it's just a reminder that we care deeply. The key is learning not to let guilt define us.

I can't even begin to count the times I've sat in my closet, bawling my eyes out, trying to catch my breath, wondering when it would get easier. How do you pick yourself up and go on with your day when your brain is stuck on worries and what-ifs? I know my girls are only young once, and I treasure every connection we have. But let's be honest, raising kids is hard. We laugh, we play, we have fun… but sometimes my mind drifts to the never-ending list of chores and tasks I need to finish.

Am I doing enough? That constant, nagging voice in the back of your mind. It shows up when you need space, lose your patience, want more than just motherhood, or simply don't love every single moment. It's heavy, exhausting, and an all-too-common feeling that many moms carry in silence. But why? Why do we let it take over?

Mom guilt can sound like:

"I shouldn't have yelled."

"I miss my old life, is that awful?"

"I'm tired of playing. Does that make me a bad mom?"

"I want to exercise, but I can't because I have kids."

"I love this kid-free night, but what if they need me?"

"Why do I want time away from my kids?"

"I chose to be a mom, I shouldn't complain."

You may have said some of these to yourself or out loud. Feeling this doesn't make you a bad mom. It makes you honest.

Listen, mama, I get it. I've been there. I'm still there at times. Deep down, the guilt is because we care. We want to get it right, to be the perfect mom. And that's beautiful. Striving for the best is one thing; letting guilt control you is another.

Let's be honest. You may take thirty minutes to read a book while your spouse or a caregiver watches the kids. Five minutes in, one is screaming, the other is running up and down the stairs calling for you, and you feel that pull to drop everything and "fix it." That guilt sneaks in. Maybe my kids need me more right now. NO! You asked for this time because you needed it.

Then there's social media. The perfectly staged reels, the family smiling around a spotless kitchen, the immaculate home, while dinner is cooking. We don't see the meltdowns, the loneliness, or the mental load that goes on behind the scenes. But we compare ourselves anyway. Am I doing enough? What am I doing wrong? That self-criticism feeds guilt.

And let's not forget generational expectations. Many of us were raised by women who "did it all without complaint"—and were simply expected to. The message sticks: *This is the life you chose, so you must sacrifice everything.* But just because that's how things were done decades ago doesn't mean it's your only option. Times have changed. Resources have changed. Work-from-home opportunities, flexible schedules, and modern parenting tools allow you to choose differently. You birthed these babies—you get to raise them in the way that best suits your life.

When it comes to parenting, there's no clock-out, no performance review, no recognition for "a job well done." Just you, wondering if you've done enough. Working moms, stay-at-home moms, mompreneurs, it doesn't matter. You're always on the clock. Your kid gets sick; you juggle work and care. You want a night out; you feel the need to plan everything for your spouse or sitter. Your phone goes off; your brain jumps to the worst-case scenario. And all of this? It feeds the mom guilt.

What I've realized is that guilt is often a reflection of unrealistic expectations, not actual wrongdoing. You are allowed to be a full human being, not just a selfless caretaker. Needing time, space, or support doesn't make you a bad mom. It makes you human. Instead of thinking, "I feel guilty for taking time for myself," try reframing it as "My needs matter too, and meeting them helps me show up better for others."

Let's call mom guilt what it really is—an emotional burden that most moms carry silently. Heavy. Exhausting. And often completely unrealistic. It's that constant pressure to be everything for everyone. The emotionally available, always-calm parent. The spotless-home manager. The partner, cook, chauffeur, scheduler, nurse, and teacher all rolled into one. The "present" and "perfect" mom who somehow has no needs of her own. This burden doesn't come with a handbook. There's no training, no warning, no pause button. It creeps in during the quiet moments when you're folding laundry or cleaning up spilled snacks, and it whispers that you're not doing enough. It hits when you finally steal ten minutes for yourself and immediately feel guilty that your kids aren't getting "perfect mom" in that moment.

These perfect expectations are impossible to meet. Carrying them silently only makes them heavier. This is why so many of us feel drained, isolated, and like we're failing, even when we're doing our absolute best. But acknowledging it is the first step toward freedom. When you name the guilt, you take some of its power away. When you recognize it, you can start shifting your mindset, setting boundaries, and giving yourself the grace you've been denying yourself for too long. You deserve to be more than the sum of your roles. You deserve to feel joy without guilt, to take space without apology, and to embrace the messy, beautiful chaos without thinking it reflects on your worth as a mom.

Here's how we can change the mom guilt narrative:

- **Acknowledge your guilt:** Write down why you feel guilty. Awareness is the first step to healing.

- **Focus on connection, not perfection:** Your kids don't need a perfect mom—they need a present, loving, growing mom who models self-love.

- **Take breaks, unapologetically:** Resting isn't abandoning your family. It preserves your ability to show up fully. Even ten to thirty minutes to breathe, meditate, read, or walk matters.

- **Practice self-compassion:** Would you speak to your best friend the way you speak to yourself in your lowest "mom moments?" No. You deserve that same softness.

You are allowed to mess up. You are allowed to feel joy and fulfillment outside of your kids. Take that fitness class. Have that night out. Leave your phone in your bag. Mom guilt doesn't decide your worth; you do.

Heart-to-Self Moment

What is the most common thing I feel guilty about and why?

I feel guilty for:

What is one way I can offer myself more grace this week?

One way I can offer myself more grace is:

What unrealistic expectations do I have for myself? How can I identify which ones are realistic and which aren't?

The expectations I place on myself are:

CHAPTER NINE

The Unspoken Burdens of Resentment

Why the Little Things Start to Hurt

I didn't realize resentment could lie inside love. I've been reflecting on the moments that felt heavy, discouraging, and full of rage. The number of times I've sat on the floor of my closet with the door closed, bawling my eyes out because I was so overwhelmed... It's more than I'd ever admit out loud. But I kept those moments hidden. I reminded myself that I am lucky, I have a beautiful family, two healthy girls, and a roof over my head. No one needed to see the struggle because I knew I would pick myself back up. And more importantly, I never wanted my daughters to see me so upset. Maybe you've had your own closet-floor moment too, the meltdown no one sees, the tears you wipe away before anyone notices. You can love your children fiercely and still feel resentful of the weight you're carrying. Both emotions can exist at once.

At one point, I became obsessed with keeping everything tidy and clean... or at least making it look that way. The playroom had to be cleaned every night so the toys wouldn't be all over the place. Beds needed to be made because there's a calming feeling going to bed at night when your bed looks peaceful. The floor had to be spotless —no crumbs to prevent ants from taking over the kitchen. I told myself it was all in the name of teaching responsibility, but really, I was desperate to feel in control. After a while, I felt utterly overwhelmed by it all, like no one was there to help me stay afloat. Resentment grows quietly, like a vine wrapping around your heart until you can barely breathe. And when you bottle it all up? The resentment doesn't disappear. It compounds.

I stopped doing my husband's dishes if he left them on the counter. Why couldn't he just put them in the sink after I had just finished cleaning it? And don't even get me started on the empty containers he'd bring home from work days later. The rage was real.

Every relationship is different, and every family has its own rhythm. Yet so often, moms become the "default parent," the one who manages the household, sacrifices personal time or career goals, and carries the brunt of childcare. The mental load can feel relentless: juggling schedules, remembering appointments, running errands, planning meals, and even caring for pets. Add pregnancy, postpartum recovery, and the challenge of loving a body that feels foreign, and it's no wonder resentment quietly slips in.

Sometimes your partner has a demanding job, leaving more childcare and household responsibilities on your shoulders. You spend the day decoding cries, tantrums, backtalk, and endless messes. Your partner comes home to a disaster, even though you've cleaned twice already. Then comes dinner, cleanup, and the bedtime routine that takes at least forty-five minutes. Finally, the kids are asleep, and all you want is to collapse on the couch and zone out to Netflix. Thirty seconds later, you're asleep. Goodnight, world.

Not everyone has family nearby or alternative childcare options, so we end up doing everything ourselves. Between chores, meltdowns, problem-solving, appointments, and endless to-do lists, asking for help can feel like more work than it's worth. So, we stay silent, push through, and carry the weight, quietly. I used to tell myself to just be grateful and not complain. I avoided asking for help because it meant explaining what needed to be done, and sometimes it felt easier just to do it myself. But resentment builds quickly when our effort feels invisible.

I remember weekends when my husband would text me while I was out, asking what to feed the kids. My blood would boil. Part of me wanted to shout, part of me wanted to laugh. I love him dearly, but in that moment, I'd think, "I don't know, maybe open the fridge? When you're at work, I don't call to ask what to feed the kids, I just figure it out."

Let's be real here. Sometimes the resentment we feel isn't even about the what's-for-dinner questions, the dishes, or the laundry. It's about the feeling of always being the default parent. My daughter will come to me to say she has to go to the bathroom when she was literally standing right next to my husband. And when I'm busy cooking, sautéing onions, putting butternut squash in the oven, and cubing the chicken, they still call my name for a glass of milk. I'm the one who has to think for everyone, remember everything, and still keep the household together without falling apart. There's an expectation that I'm supposed to just "know" what we need.

If my girls spend the night out, I'm in charge of packing their bags. It's not that my husband isn't capable of doing it, but he'll end up asking me where everything is. Or he'll pack an outfit that makes no sense. At this point I'm convinced he knows where things are… he just enjoys watching me find them faster. Maybe he just knows I like to stay active, so he pretends not to know where anything is. It all falls back on me. All the birthdays to remember, how to "gentle parent," and keeping milk stocked in the fridge.

It becomes exhausting.

Irritation grows, and then the snapping over little things starts. You feel like you're failing, but you're actually fighting to handle it all, keep the sparks alive, make sure the house feels safe for your kids, and create lots of happy childhood memories.

Isn't it crazy how motherhood can feel lonely, especially when you're never actually alone? The number of times I sat in my car in the Target parking lot wiping my tears. Checking my eyes to make sure they aren't puffy or red before I leave my car. If I walk inside, I could see a friend or someone I know. They don't need to see me like this. I don't want to feel this way, but there are moments I do. I don't want to feel like I'm the manager of the house. I want to be seen and heard and not simply relied upon until I break down.

Resentment isn't a failure; it's a signal. It's a reminder that you need support, boundaries, and grace. When you start honoring your needs and speaking up, you reclaim a piece of your life, your energy, and your joy. Once I started "letting go," I realized how much pressure I'd placed on myself, believing I was the only one who could do things "right". How did I get here? Gosh, I'm still trying to figure that out fully.

Letting go sounds simple, but it's uncomfortable. It means admitting I don't have to be the default for everything. Trusting that things might get done differently than I would do them, and damn, that in itself is hard. I've realized that even when someone else takes on the task, I'm still mentally involved: thinking it through, explaining it, overseeing it. I'm not physically doing the work, but I haven't actually let it go.

So how can we work on dismantling resentment?

Here's what helps:

Speak up about your needs. Communicate honestly with your partner, family, or support system.

I started asking my husband to handle bedtime so I can decompress on days I'm feeling built up to the max. We also talk about whether events actually fit into our schedule without overwhelming ourselves before saying yes. We're paying more attention to what fits our life instead of forcing everything in.

Renegotiate roles and responsibilities. Find small ways to share the load.

My husband is now in charge of dinner on Tuesday nights. This allows me to drive the girls to and from school and activities without rushing to make dinner, and we can walk out the door to play volleyball together when our sitter comes. Is dinner always ready on time? No. Do I sometimes silently scream while reminding myself to breathe? Absolutely. But it's still one less thing I'm responsible for, and that alone feels like a win. Now I just let him handle it. (This is love. This is marriage. This is teamwork... with a side of patience.)

Create space where your needs come first. Your priorities matter, too.

Like taking a shower without rushing, even if it means the laundry waits. On Sundays, I enjoy going to the coffee shop to grab coffee for my husband and a latte or cappuccino for myself. There are times I sit in my car for a few quiet minutes before walking into the house, or blasting Icona Pop's "I Don't Care" and singing my heart out. I read a few pages from a book instead of scrolling on my phone, and I wake up early for a quick workout because it makes me feel good.

Set boundaries to protect your energy. You can't pour from an empty cup.

Letting a text sit unanswered until I have the energy or time to respond has been a game-changer. I may see a text come through, but if I know in the moment I cannot get to it, there's no point in trying to read it. If something is truly urgent, a phone call will follow. I think we all know what *urgent* means, not "Hey, can you send me that link real quick?"

Ask for help and let it be enough. Releasing control doesn't mean things won't get done.

There are some areas I do like organized a certain way. But if the playroom is cleaned up and there aren't tiny Barbie shoes, pots from the play kitchen, and puzzle pieces on the floor, that's a win. They might be thrown in a bin with the Magna-tiles, but hey, they are cleaned up, and I didn't have to do it. (I'm just thinking in the back of my mind that I'll reorganize it another day.)

And let me be clear: I am not the only problem. We moms are not imagining this weight, and we're not the sole reason resentment shows up. Healing resentment isn't just about us learning to let go or communicate better. Sometimes, it's about our partners stepping up and getting their shit together too.

Because self-awareness is great, but it doesn't unload the dishwasher. Growth is wonderful, but it doesn't magically teach someone where the socks go. This is a team effort. And while I'm working on releasing control and asking for help, the people around me also have to meet me halfway, preferably without asking where everything is while standing directly in front of it.

If you use a calendar for all your family activities or work events, what if you blocked off time for yourself? Even just ten minutes can go a long way. Planning your days out can help you get a clearer sense of the time you have. Even small shifts, like delegating one night a week, have made a difference and given me a little break. That basket of laundry that's sitting in the hallway, there's no harm in asking for help with it. I started playing a game with the kids to find the matching socks. I know it won't be perfect, but it starts the process for me. Even asking my husband to fold the towels checks things off my list. The other day, I opened my closet to find that he had even rolled them the way I like.

None of this is about doing things perfectly. It's about recognizing that support doesn't have to look the same every day to matter. Every time I ask for help, delegate a task, or let go of doing it "my way," I reclaim a little more space for myself. And that space is where my patience, energy, and joy start to return.

Heart-to-Self Moment

Where in my life do I feel underreported or unseen?
I feel unseen when:

Is there a person or situation in my life that is causing resentment? How can I communicate my feelings more openly?

What are some overwhelming tasks I can "let go" of, allowing others to step in and help me?
The tasks I can release are:

CHAPTER TEN

Reconnecting With Your Identity Outside of "Mom"

Learning to Take up Space Again

Motherhood shapes a new identity: MOM—the one who is patient, productive, gentle, fit, on-the-go, and present. Our minds live in demand mode, even when our bodies are supposed to be resting.

We hear the words "Mom," or "babe," or our first name hundreds of times a day because someone needs us, wants us, or is waiting on us. And even when we don't hear it out loud, we swear we do. It's like when you're in the shower and think you hear your name being called. You open the door, only to realize it's completely quiet. It's the constant mental soundtrack: go here, do this, help with that, what's today, what's tomorrow, "Mom, can I have a snack?"

I'll sit down for what I confidently tell myself will be a ten-minute break, only to pop back up two minutes later. No one asked me to. No one needed anything. My brain just panicked and said, "Relaxing feels wrong, you should check on everyone." That's motherhood. Even when we stop moving, our minds are still clocked in.

We all put our hobbies on pause because we prioritize our kids. There's nothing wrong with that, no shame in it, but when it happens constantly, it consumes us. We get stuck in a rhythm that feels messy, unorganized, and overwhelming, yet somehow we make it work. Every day starts to feel like an endless cycle: wake up, throw on joggers, make breakfast, forget to eat yourself because there's no time. We allow ourselves to set our needs aside, keeping everyone else happy, even when deep down, we're crying out for more. Yes, you're a mom, but you're also: a woman, a dreamer, a lover of all things beyond diapers, schedules, and school pick-ups. That version of you may feel buried, but she's not gone.

Let me say this loud and clear: Your worth has never left you. It's just buried under the noise.

Reconnecting with yourself isn't selfish; it's sacred. You deserve to feel whole, not just as a mom, but as a person. This teaches our kids the importance of balance. We are their moms, but we also have our own name, our own identity. We can be both. That little voice inside that says, "They need me, or they'll fail," is wrong. Our kids need a mom who is her best self— healthy, confident, and empowered. How can we teach them to pursue their dreams if we aren't pursuing ours?

Reconnecting with yourself as a whole person, not just as a mom, is essential to your emotional well-being, your identity, and your long-term happiness. It's time to stop hiding behind the curtains and start showing up for yourself the same way you show up for everyone else. Those dreams you once had, the relationships that may have faded, the parts of you that feel disconnected, they're still within reach. You don't have to wait for the perfect moment or for the fast-paced world to settle. You can start right now, one small, intentional step at a time.

Here are ten grounded and empowering tips to help you come back to "you":

1. Reclaim Time That's Just Yours

Even if it's only ten or fifteen minutes a day, set aside time that belongs entirely to you, not your kids, not your partner, not anyone else. It doesn't have to be productive; it just needs to be *yours*. Schedule it on your calendar, set a reminder, and take it seriously because you matter, too. That book that's been sitting on your nightstand? Here's your moment to read a few pages. Step outside, get some sunlight, and move your body. This can be as simple as sitting on your patio while the sun rises, or taking a morning walk while the light glows softly on your face. Maybe there's a workout class you've been wanting to try, so sign up and go! The key is to make the time and then actually use it. Don't cancel your own plans because someone else might need you. You're doing this because you need you.

2. Revisit What Lights You Up

Think back to what inspired you before motherhood: music, writing, painting, running, photography, etc. Revisit it. That part of you still exists and deserves attention. I joined local volleyball leagues. And please do not come at me with the "you're too old" comments. You can absolutely still do things you did when you were younger or right before having kids.

Maybe you loved making pottery and want to get back into it. Or perhaps you've always had a passion for flowers and arranging them beautifully. Follow that spark. In fact, the amazing thing about the world we live in now is that you can often turn those passions into something more, maybe even a small business or side hustle that fills you with purpose. And if you're sitting here thinking, "I don't know what I like anymore..." you are not alone. As our identity shifts, so many things we once loved feel out of reach. Now is a great time to let your curiosity shine and try things.

3. Practice Saying "I" Without Guilt

You're allowed to say things like:

"I need a break."

"I want to be alone for a bit."

"I miss who I was."

"I want a night out."

"I don't want to go."

This matters. This is still your life to live and your journey. When you feel happy and energized, those feelings are contagious and bring that same vibe to your home. What if your day started with, "I worked out with no disruptions," or "I sat on the couch with a hot cup of coffee and listened to a book," or "I'm going to Target ALONE"? Imagine the shift in your mood and in your entire household's mood. It's okay to let "I" become part of your vocabulary again.

4. Journal Without a Filter

Write not as a mom, but as you. Begin with prompts like: What do I miss about myself?
How is my life expanding and changing? What am I longing for?
Your journal is your space, your place to say whatever you want. You can write first thing in the morning

or at night while lying in bed. It's all about what works best for you. I'll admit, I don't journal every day. But for three months I did, and I noticed a real difference in myself. In the morning, I wrote down just three goals for the day so I wouldn't feel overwhelmed or try to cram everything in. It gave me space to put my feelings on paper and get them off my chest. At night, I reflected on something positive that happened.

Let me emphasize this: *Always list the positive things from your day. It's easy to get caught up in the negatives and forget that some good always comes out of the day.*

5. Get Back into Your Body

Motherhood often makes you feel like a machine. Constantly moving, endlessly giving. But your body is so much more than that. Reconnect with yourself through movement that honors your physical self: yoga, walking, dancing, stretching, or anything that reminds you that you have a body beyond caregiving.

Movement is so important for our physical and mental health, and it relieves some stress. You don't need to be fully dressed in a Lululemon outfit with your hair in a braid. You don't even need to spend hours at the gym with the right playlist and no interruptions. Make it simple. Go for a walk while pushing your little one in a stroller, stretch on the floor while your kids climb on you, or do a twenty to thirty-minute workout in your living room.

There are days when I work out in my basement, where all my dumbbells, bands, and kettlebells are. Other days, I am in the living room doing a fifteen-minute high-intensity workout with no equipment while my kids eat breakfast. I also have a pair of dumbbells and booty bands in my office that I can pull out at any time. My workouts are not an hour long, and they are usually interrupted. But I still get something done. It matters.

If you aren't happy with how you are feeling and want to be more energized for your family, say YES to moving your body. Say YES to strength. Say YES to ten minutes to start. Not just because you want to "bounce back," but because you want to feel good in your own skin. Your body has carried you through every moment of motherhood. Now it's time to give it the love and attention it deserves.

And if you're looking for someone to lovingly kick your butt into gear... hi, it's me.

6. Connect with Other Moms—Or Those with Similar Interests

Motherhood changes your social circle. As moms, we often text each other or talk about the tantrums our kids are having, trying to determine what is considered "normal." Of course, having kids naturally brings you closer to other moms and dads who are on a similar journey. That connection is valuable; you understand each other and can share laughs about the challenges you're facing. But don't forget to nurture the social parts of your life beyond parenting. Make space for conversations that aren't about kids. Reach out to friends who knew you before motherhood, or build new friendships that connect with other parts of who you are.

And yes, this can feel awkward at first. Friendships change. Some drift apart, others grow stronger, and new ones appear in seasons you didn't expect. That's normal. You're not doing anything wrong, you're evolving.

I remember going on what I like to call a "mom date." A friend connected me with another mom she had met, knowing we shared similar interests. Our first meet-up was at a playground over the summer, and we instantly hit it off. We were in similar seasons of motherhood, both loved fitness, both were passionate about empowering women, and somehow managed to enjoy cider at an orchard with our kids running around. It reminded me that friendships don't disappear after motherhood, they just look different.

And if meeting someone new feels intimidating, start online. There are so many mom groups on social media where women connect over parenting, fitness, hobbies, and everyday life. Sometimes all it takes is one message or comment to spark a real friendship. From there, it can be as simple as meeting up at a playground, going for a walk with the kids, or grabbing coffee while they play.

Take a girls' trip. And please stop convincing yourself you can't. Every automatic no builds another wall between you and the version of you you're rebuilding. Join a fitness class with a friend. Plan a day trip to the beach. Sit at a coffee shop and vent about your spouse or just life in general. Everyone loves a good therapy session! Being surrounded by like-minded friends helps bring out the best in you and lets you be your unfiltered self. It's amazing how just an hour or so of adult conversation can help you feel recharged, more patient, and more yourself. Motherhood is just a chapter in your story, not the entire book. All relationships have room to grow, so surround yourself with those who support you, make you feel seen, and remind you that you are doing amazing. Nurture those friendships and interests that remind you of YOU.

7. Practice Saying "No" to Others (So You Can Say "Yes" to Yourself)

Protect your energy by learning to say no to obligations that drain you. Every time you say no, you create space for your own voice to return. I noticed a profound difference in myself when I realized it was okay to say no if I didn't want to do something. You don't need to please everyone. Saying no isn't selfish; it's an act of self-awareness. It's choosing self-worth over burnout. When you honor your time, your energy, and your values, you eliminate what no longer serves you. This creates room for personal growth, passion, and relationships that truly bring joy and meaning to your life.

Let's take a moment to reflect. What have you said yes to recently that you regretted? Have you felt obligated to do things that don't excite you? Next time you're asked something that you're going back and forth with, try pausing before responding. You don't owe anyone an answer right away. One thing I am still working on is saying no without feeling the need to explain my reasoning to avoid being judged.

8. Create Something Just for You

Whether it's a small DIY project, a vision board, a playlist, or even learning a new skill, creating something solely for yourself helps you reclaim your creativity and autonomy. I personally love DIY projects! My husband, on the other hand, isn't much of a fan. He's just not as creative as I am and doesn't have an eye for crafts. (Sorry, Bae, if you're reading this!) But for me, creating things or painting brings me happiness and a deep sense of calm.

It doesn't have to be a big production or presentation; make it whatever you want. For years, I told myself I wanted to write a book. I had ideas, but could never quite sit down and fully focus on them. When I finally made the conscious choice to "make time" for myself, the magic happened.

This book began as a simple outlet to express my feelings in the moment, but it has grown into something so much more. Most importantly, it's something that is mine. I created it. I had these stories, ideas, and moments I knew other moms could relate to. I made the time to get my writing in and spent countless days at the cafe writing while my girls were at school. I could have driven straight home and done some house chores, but that's no fun. I would rather push them off and let myself have the fulfilling writing time.

Here are a few examples of small, creative projects you can do:

- Start a scrapbook
- Plant a garden
- Find new recipes and create your own book of recipes
- Write a book
- Take a dance class just for fun
- Start a morning or evening routine
- Try crocheting or knitting
- Learn to play an instrument
- Paint by numbers artwork.

- Start your own Etsy page, especially if you enjoy being creative with coffee mugs, t-shirts, bags, etc.

These little projects that you take on start to remind you that you are more than the task you complete. You are a creator, a thinker, someone capable of having passions that deserve space. You may find something that starts small and grows into something healing.

9. Let Go of the "Perfect Mom" Narrative

The pressure to "do it all" and "be it all" can suffocate your individual identity. It's time to let it go. Being real and whole is far better than chasing an impossible ideal. Seriously, aren't you tired of chasing perfection? It's exhausting.

I know I've touched on this before in the book, but it bears repeating: your kids don't need a perfect mom. They don't even know what that looks like. What they want is to see you, authentic, honest, vulnerable, and human. They don't need flawless meals, spotless kitchens, or toys organized by color, shape, and size. They don't need a mom who never loses her patience or always knows what she's doing.

Letting go of perfection allows you to embrace presence, joy, and authenticity in the belly laughs, the mess, the imperfect meals, and the chaotic schedules. The more we try to control every piece of motherhood, the more we lose the magic of it. Your kids will most remember how you made them feel—safe, loved, and seen. I can assure you my kids do not care that I did a load of laundry and it's still sitting in the basket a few days later. If I make pancakes and they go everywhere, they think it's hilarious. (I would too if I weren't the one cleaning it up.)

Replace "Am I doing enough?" with "I AM enough." Celebrate your efforts over Pinterest-perfect images, and connection over comparison. Your best is more than enough.

10. Contemplate Who You Are Becoming

You're not the same person you were before motherhood—and that's more than okay. Reconnecting with yourself doesn't mean going backward; it means being curious about the person you're evolving into. Every day, you have the chance to make choices for yourself. How incredible is that?

Before motherhood, maybe you were spontaneous and said yes to every plan, or perhaps you were still figuring out who you were. Then motherhood came, and suddenly the things that mattered to you shifted. Yes, our kids are a big part of our lives, but they do not define who we are. Motherhood doesn't limit us; it opens the door to designing the version of ourselves we want to become.

This could mean something as big as a career change or as simple as finding new routines that align with your goals and values. Maybe you start a side business during nap times. Maybe you change your morning routine to suit you and your needs better. Maybe you volunteer, or maybe you write a book (like I did, without realizing it).

Sure, our kids need their mom when they're sick, have accidents, or feel overwhelmed, but that's not all we are. And, yes, you will think, Shouldn't I be home? Shouldn't I be doing something more productive for my family? But you will also feel lighter, more patient, and more yourself. Motherhood changes us, but it can also make us feel stronger, more alive, and more intentional than ever before. Embrace this new you. Discover what lights you up and pursue it with passion.

You know that journaling I mentioned? Here are some affirmations you can write down and repeat to yourself. You can use that moment you are finally alone in the bathroom after a warm shower to say these out loud, or you can write them on sticky notes and place them around your space as daily reminders. Here are a few examples to help get you started:

I am becoming intentional with my priorities and how I spend my time.

I am becoming confident, trusting myself without seeking approval.

I am becoming authentic, showing up for myself, even when it's messy.

I am becoming present with my surroundings.

I am becoming HER, but stronger this time.

Take a moment and ask yourself, "Who am I becoming?" Write down the first answer that comes to mind without editing it. Let this answer guide you forward.

Heart-to-Self Moment

What makes me feel confident or alive?
I feel alive when I allow myself to:

What parts of my identity feel lost or muted?
One part of myself I've pushed aside is:

What is one thing I love about myself? I can be my own
biggest critic, but I still hold something personal and
unique to myself.
One thing I truly love about who I am is:

CHAPTER ELEVEN

Trust the Process
You're Not Doing it Wrong—It's Just Hard

You might be thinking, "What the hell, Elyse? How am I supposed to just drop everything and focus on myself when I can't even pee alone?" And, fair. But all I'm really asking you to do is remember that you matter. I'm simply showing you what you're capable of and giving you permission to take time for yourself. No, you don't have to run off at sunrise to grab a cappuccino and journal, but I also won't stop you!

That woman you were before motherhood was beautiful and full of life, but she didn't know what you know now. This point is accepting that you're not going back, and that you're not meant to. This acceptance won't happen overnight, and there's no switch you can flip. It's not about waking up one morning and suddenly feeling your best. It's a process—slow, quiet, messy, exciting, and sometimes terrifying.

We are here, rewriting our identity from the inside out, finding hobbies, creating spaces, and moving our bodies because it makes us feel alive. Some days, reclaiming yourself will feel absolutely amazing. You'll go to that yoga or strength training class, book yourself a spa day, take a girls' trip, or even change careers. Other days will bring tears, restless nights, and tragedies. It's like rebuilding the home you once lived in, but making it your own again. Setting boundaries that serve you and your family, saying yes to what heals you.

This journey you're on? It's going to feel hard AF. There's also a fear of being judged for choosing yourself, for wanting more. But if taking control of my life and creating a joyful environment for myself and my kids seems selfish to some... who cares? We get one shot at life, and I don't know about you, but I'm done wasting it on what other people think about me and my choices.

I hit a point in my own motherhood journey where I decided things needed to change. I realized, this is still my life. My story is still being written. The pieces that felt missing? It was up to me to find them. I spent so much time preaching confidence to others, and I finally had to take my own advice.

I started voicing my feelings instead of burying them. If I needed help, I asked for it. And if it didn't happen when I asked? Well, I'm still working on that patience. (I know you get it.) When I feel overwhelmed, I step back, breathe deep, and handle one thing at a time.

I started finding joy in reading and listening to audiobooks again. Books became my reset button. They let my mind escape the noise, even if it was just while I folded laundry or hid in the bathroom pretending to poop. I was rediscovering the woman who loved stories long before motherhood filled every corner of her life—one chapter, one quiet moment at a time.

And speaking of the bathroom, shoutout to my husband, who somehow disappears in there for thirty uninterrupted minutes while I'm juggling snacks, spills, and sibling fights. One day, I decided I deserved that same energy. So, I took my book and my fake bathroom break upstairs. Ten minutes later? Kids banging on the door. Husband calling, "What are you doing?"
Sir... I'm taking. My. Shit. At least give me the same thirty-minute courtesy! (This is a secret between us moms: use the system to your advantage.) That became my boundary. Not huge. Not life-changing. But mine.

Then, in January of 2025, I started journaling every morning and night. To start my day, I wrote down three tiny goals, like:

- Clean for thirty minutes
- Read ten pages of my book
- Move my body for 20 minutes
- Complete 1 load of laundry (wash, dry and put away)
- Meal Prep
- Record 5 exercises for my workout program
- Try something new today

- Make someone smile today
- Organize 1 room

At night, I wrote down the good stuff from my day:
- My daughter hugged me out of nowhere
- Hubby cooked dinner (hell yeah)
- A moment of peace I created for myself
- I read for thirty minutes, uninterrupted
- Had my ass kicked in a workout, but it felt great
- My daughters played so well together; just watching them together brings joy
- A morning brunch with friends

Journaling helped me set boundaries and spend my energy on what matters more than spotless floors. I simplified my schedule. Laundry had a dedicated day—every other week was the kids' clothes, then ours. Simple. Sustainable.

Cooking has always been a part of who I am, and getting back into creating recipes reminded me that I'm a woman who loves flavor, creativity, and feeding others with joy. There's something about chopping vegetables, seasoning to taste, and seeing a meal come together that reminds me I'm capable of more than just surviving the day. It's calming, creative, and it's mine. My family and friends know that for every holiday or gathering, I'm always whipping up something new or bringing over my popular dishes.

I started paying attention to the woman behind the mother. And she was still in there, exhausted, yes, but awakening. I learned that strength isn't doing everything yourself.

It's admitting when you can't and asking for help to get it done anyway. I'm still working on patience. Still learning to let go. Still practicing taking a breath before reacting. Still fighting the instinct to prove I'm not "lazy." But something has shifted. I'm finding my voice. Not the whisper begging for a break, the one that says, "I deserve to enjoy my life too."

Hard truth coming at you: waiting for "someday" keeps you stuck.

Change doesn't happen in big, dramatic moments. It happens in the smallest choices, the ones where you finally decide you matter too.

Start with one tiny shift. Decide on one thing you will no longer apologize for. If your husband can disappear in the bathroom for thirty minutes, you damn well can take ten for yourself. Go find HER.

What I've learned through this beautiful mess is that being a mom doesn't mean losing yourself. It means getting the chance to rediscover who you truly are, piece by piece.

It's okay to evolve, to change your dreams, to redefine your priorities, and to admit when something no longer feels right. Amid the noise, exhaustion, and guilt, I began to catch glimpses of myself again in the quiet moments, in the laughter, and in the small victories no one else sees. I kept reaching for her, only to realize she was never gone. That woman inside me was waiting for me to slow down, listen, and choose her again. You are brave enough to rewrite your story, even if it means letting go of the past and old chapters.

Do I still make mistakes? Absolutely. But I don't see myself as a bad mom, and I don't fight the urge to want more. Each day is a new chance to live fully, to create my life, and to share my love with my family. I work on myself, not just for me, but so my kids can see it too. They need me to be present, healthy, and laughing. When the sun hits my face, I want my smile to glow. I choose happiness.

This journey isn't just about being a mom; it's about finding the woman inside you again. While some days she feels buried under all the responsibilities, she is also the one who gets you through all the hard times. And yet, let's never forget, we are moms. How incredible is it that we get to raise these kids as our own, in our own unique way? We get to show them our world, and they get to show us theirs, from tiny little feet to princess dresses, to hundreds of toys scattered across the floor and hair covered in yogurt. These moments are precious.

When my kids ask me to stay and lie in bed with them for five more minutes, I do it because they want me near. Something about little hands touching my face when they see me cry and ask what's wrong—it's an unparalleled sense of love and connection we have. Just asking for a hug and having those tiny arms try to wrap around my body is pure joy. While there's loud noise and shit everywhere, there's also joy, laughter, and love. When my daughters hug me and say, "Mom, I love you," it doesn't matter how lost I felt earlier. Their voices remind me that I am seen. They appreciate all that I do, and they feel safe.

I want my girls to watch me live authentically and be true to myself. They gave me the chance to be a mom. (Not me sitting here crying as I wrote that sentence). Motherhood didn't take me away from myself; it led me back home, in a different, more powerful form.

Our kids will grow up. We will get older, but that doesn't mean our lives pause. Don't ever tell yourself it's too late or that you're not strong enough. You absolutely freakin' are. When you look at yourself in the mirror, the woman staring back at you is your biggest fan. She's rooting for you to find your way, to celebrate the wins, and to reach out her hand when you're drowning. There will be curveballs. There will be strikeouts. But every setback is an invitation to return to yourself. Each time you stand back up, you rediscover the woman you were before the world shrank to you. She's still there, waiting for you to choose her—the one who knows you're meant for more.

Ladies, you get one shot at this life, one chance to live it fully and on your own terms, not buried under guilt, expectations, or waiting for the "right time" to finally choose yourself.

Be gentle with yourself. With every breath, every boundary, every small moment you choose peace over perfection, she comes closer into view. Maybe that looks like drinking your coffee while it's still hot, or lacing up your shoes for a workout, even if the house is a mess. Remember: you get to play with your kids. You get to go to that fitness class. You get to go to dinner with your girlfriends. You get to say no.

If you're reading this, wishing you could be brave, you already are. It's not easy, but it's not impossible. Picture yourself a year from now, what do you envision your life to be like? Do you see yourself more at ease and your voice heard? Maybe you imagine a future something like this:

> You wake up and feel empowered to take on the day.

> You don't sprint into survival mode or jump right into the chaos.

You create time for yourself to drink your coffee or get a workout in.

You speak up and express your feelings.

You say "I" without shrinking.

You chase things that light you up.

You plan nights out with friends.

You have a hobby that brings you joy.

You smile, laugh, and live freely.

It's all possible! That woman who has been whispering has finally made her way to the surface. Take a second, close your eyes, and take a deep breath in. Exhale and let it all out.

Here's to you, the mom, the woman, the dreamer. Here's to embracing the chaos and savoring the calm. To laughing, loving, and living fully, even when it's messy. You don't have to choose between being a mom and being yourself; you get to be both. Today, choose YOU. Reclaim your time, your joy, your passions. Shine unapologetically. Because when you honor yourself, you show your kids how to do the same. This is your life. Your story. Your beautiful, imperfect, powerful journey. Own it.

And now, I want to leave you with this: you don't have to do everything I did, or do it the way I did it. Your version of choosing yourself will look different, and that's exactly how it should be. But I hope you walk away knowing this: you are allowed to want more, to rest, to change, and to take up space in your own life. Your story doesn't end here. It begins again every time you choose yourself.

Grab your cup of coffee, sparkling water, glass of wine, or bottle of beer, and let's make a toast to being human, feeling deeply, changing our minds, and choosing ourselves, unapologetically.

Heart-to-Self Moment

What is one small boundary I can set to protect my peace?
One boundary I need to start practicing is:

What does "choosing myself" look like in this season of life?
Right now, choosing myself means:

What old version of me am I grateful for, and what new
version am I becoming?
I honor the woman I was because:

I'm becoming the woman who:

She's already in there.

I can't wait for you to meet her.

CHAPTER TWELVE

Paying it All Forward
Finding Yourself and Guiding the Next Generation

If you're still here, it means something in these pages felt familiar. Maybe you saw yourself in the exhaustion, the guilt, the wanting more without knowing what "more" even looks like. If you're still here, I want to start by saying thank you. Not just for reading these pages, but for staying with yourself while you did. Because I know this book probably stirred things up. Maybe it brought comfort. Maybe it made you feel seen. Or maybe it cracked open feelings you've been pushing down for a long time because there simply hasn't been space to deal with them.

This book was never meant to give you answers. It was meant to remind you that you're not alone in the questions.

If you've learned anything from my story, I hope it's this: losing yourself doesn't mean you're broken. It means you've been pouring into everyone else for a long time. And finding yourself again doesn't require a dramatic overhaul or a perfectly planned life. It starts with noticing. With honesty. With small choices that bring you back into your own body, your own thoughts, your own wants.

If this book has shown you anything, I hope it's that becoming her again isn't about going back to who you were before motherhood. That woman didn't know what you know now. She hadn't been stretched, challenged, or reshaped by love the way you have. This isn't about returning, it's about evolving, about meeting yourself where you are and deciding to move forward with intention instead of guilt. And when you close it, don't rush into the next thing. Sit for a moment. Take a breath. Ask yourself one simple question: What do I need right now?

When I finished writing the first draft of the book, I realized the importance of this message isn't just for new moms. One day, my daughters may decide to have children of their own. Here I am trying to help other women, when I have two little girls right in front of me who need to hear my truth, too. They need to know my thoughts, my reasons, my choices.

There's something about writing things down, then coming back to read them. The words stick with you differently. And what if one day I'm not here to tell my girls face-to-face, I want my voice to be something they can always come back to.

That's why I started writing a letter to them so that they can read it for themselves. Writing this letter isn't about expecting the worst; it's about leaving pieces of myself behind in the best way. It's about making sure my girls always have access to my voice, my love, and my truth, no matter where life takes them.

Think how cool it would be to write a letter to your kids about who you are. Create an email address for them and send them random emails about your days together or maybe special moments. But also, acknowledge the hard times. Save the letter for their high school graduation, when they turn sixteen, or whenever you feel they're ready to read it. Pictures are great for capturing memories, but this letter will give something more. And it doesn't have to be long or poetic or beautifully written. It just has to be honest. Your kids don't need perfect words; they need *your* words.

This is my gift to them.

A Message to My Daughters: The Woman I Hope You See in Me

If your little blue eyes ever read these pages, I want you to walk away with this message that took me far too long to learn:

Your worth is in who you are. Behind the mess, the sleepless nights, the friends and family you lose, the days you question everything, never lose sight of yourself.

I hope you always chase the things that light you up.

I hope you never shrink so that others feel powerful over you.

I hope you always see the beauty in yourself.

I hope you never lower your expectations just to please others.

I want you to know that being your mother is the greatest gift I could have ever asked for. From the moment you both were born, you have given me a kind of love I never knew existed. I cherish every single moment we have together, and I will always be right by your side. But

I am a woman too, with dreams, passions, fears, and flaws. I know now that I want you to see all of that. Because one day, you will grow into women with your own desires. I hope you look at me and don't just see me as "Mom." I hope you see a woman who is brave and takes risks—a woman who is strong and encouraging.

In this life, you will break down and feel like you're suffocating, with no end in sight. But I'm here to tell you that it's okay. You may break down, but you will rebuild. And you can do it as many times as you need. You are human.

The lessons you both have taught me cannot be found in books. The day I ran the Spartan Race at Citizens Bank Park, one obstacle challenged me physically and mentally in a way I had never experienced before. I was climbing up a rope, near the end of the race, and I was so close to the top. My hands were slipping, and I remember looking up and seeing the bell. I took a deep breath and told myself, I can do this. I have to do this for my kids. I refused to give up without trying my absolute hardest. And I did it! My body was shaking from the thrill of it. All I want in life is to be the best possible role model I can be for you.

We are going to have disagreements. You'll tell me I'm wrong, we'll probably argue, but then we will bring it in for the warmest hug. The bond we have is too strong for any hurricane to shatter. There were moments you tested my patience, brought me to tears, yelled at me, and shrugged your shoulders like you wanted to ignore me. Those things hurt in the moment, but as your mom, I had to find a way to show you I'm still standing right here. I may have walked away to catch my breath, but in no way did any of that make me love you any less. It pushed limits that I didn't even know I had.

In those times when I needed space, please know that it was for me, and not a reflection of how I felt about you. I mean, I guess in those moments I was upset that you made me feel hopeless—even when I tried every gentle parenting tip possible, and you still were your defiant selves. Those few minutes to myself or that drive to Target by myself, I needed that so I could return feeling refreshed.

Life will try to pull you in every direction, but I want you both to always choose yourselves. What is going to make you happy and align with your values? You are going to upset people, I'm sure, including me, but no matter what, this is your life. And I am going to support you one hundred percent of the way.

I hope to continue empowering you girls to be your best selves. To shine brighter than the sun, and to live with your eyes and heart open. I am beyond honored to be your mom and your biggest cheerleader. If there ever comes a day when I'm not standing right beside you, I want you to hear my voice in your head, reminding you of this: You are capable. You are worthy. You have everything you need inside you to keep going.

I hope this letter finds you in whatever season you're in and reminds you that you've always been enough, exactly as you are. Dream big!

Xoxo,
Mom

Acknowledgments

To my husband:
Thank you for loving me through every version of myself, even the one still figuring herself out. For standing beside me through every season I was stretched thin and still insisting I had it handled. And thank you for giving me space to grow, even when growth meant hard conversations, uncomfortable shifts, and bigger dreams.

To my daughters:
You watched me rebuild while you were still becoming. You saw the tired days, the determined ones, and the moments I chose to keep going anyway. I hope one day you read this and understand that becoming isn't something we do once —it's something we choose again and again. You are the greatest part of my becoming.

To the women who feel like they disappeared somewhere between diapers, schedules, expectations, and survival— I see you. I was you. This book is proof that you are still in there. Stop hiding her.

And finally, to the version of me who almost talked herself out of writing this—You were scared. You were tired. You were busy.

You had laundry to fold, snacks to pack, and a hundred other reasons to wait for a "better time."

But you did it anyway.

Becoming HER Again isn't about going backward.
It's not about trying to become the woman you were before kids, before responsibilities, before life got messy.

It's about rising forward—stronger, wiser, a little more tired, but unapologetically yourself.

So roll your shoulders back, lift that chin, and walk like you own it.
Because the woman you're becoming now?
She's stronger than the one you used to be.

She's unleashed... and she's not holding back anymore.

Well...

I think I've earned a spicy margarita.

About the Author

Elyse Frank is a mom to two daughters, a certified personal trainer and women's fitness specialist, and a pre-and-postnatal certified coach who is passionate about helping women feel strong, confident, and empowered—even when they're running on cold coffee and very little sleep. She is the creator of *Becoming HER Again*, a movement rooted in the belief that motherhood doesn't erase who you are; it evolves you.

After the COVID-19 pandemic forced her brick-and-mortar fitness studio to close, Elyse transitioned to online coaching. Today, she works with clients virtually, helping them understand that you don't need hours of free time, a perfect routine, or a spotless house to feel strong and confident—just small, consistent choices that honor you. She specializes in helping women rebuild their bodies, confidence, and identity in realistic ways that fit real motherhood.

Elyse's perspective on resilience was shaped long before motherhood. After experiencing the loss of a parent at a young age, she learned firsthand how grief can fracture identity, and how intentional rebuilding can restore it. That understanding deeply influences her work today, both in fitness and in life.

When she's not training clients or writing, you'll find Elyse chasing after her daughters, playing in volleyball tournaments with her husband, competing in obstacle course races that challenge her mind and body, creating relatable social media content, and laughing through the chaos that inspired this book.

You can connect with her on Instagram @_elysefrank_.